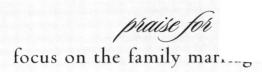

This marriage study series is pure Focus on the Family—
reliable, biblically sound and dedicated to reestablishing family values
in today's society. This series will no doubt help a multitude of couples
strengthen their relationship, not only with each other,
but also with God, the *creator* of marriage itself.

Bruce Wilkinson

Author, The BreakThrough Series: *The Prayer of Jabez,*
Secrets of the Vine and *A Life God Rewards*

In this era of such need, Dr. Dobson's team has produced solid,
helpful materials about Christian marriage. Even if they have been
through marriage studies before, every couple—married or engaged—
will benefit from this foundational study of life together. Thanks to
Focus on the Family for helping set us straight in this top priority.

Charles W. Colson

Chairman, Prison Fellowship Ministries

In my 31 years as a pastor, I've officiated at hundreds of weddings.
Unfortunately, many of those unions failed. I only wish the *Focus on the*
Family Marriage Series had been available to me during those years.
What a marvelous tool you as pastors and Christian leaders have
at your disposal. I encourage you to use it to assist those you
serve in building successful, healthy marriages.

H. B. London, Jr.

Vice President, Ministry Outreach/Pastoral Ministries
Focus on the Family

Looking for a prescription for a better marriage?
You'll enjoy this timely and practical series!

Dr. Kevin Leman

Author, *Sheet Music: Uncovering the Secrets of
Sexual Intimacy in Marriage*

The *Focus on the Family Marriage Series* is successful because it shifts
the focus from how to fix or strengthen a marriage to *who* can do it.
Through this study you will learn that a blessed marriage will be the
happy by-product of a closer relationship with the *creator* of marriage.

Lisa Whelchel

Author, *Creative Correction* and
The Facts of Life and Other Lessons My Father Taught Me

In a day and age where the covenant of marriage is so quickly tossed
aside in the name of incompatibility and irreconcilable differences, a
marriage Bible study that is both inspirational and practical is desperately
needed. The *Focus on the Family Marriage Series* is what couples are seeking.
I give my highest recommendation to this Bible study series that has the
potential to dramatically impact and improve marriages today. Marriage
is not so much about finding the right partner as it is about being the
right partner. These studies give wonderful biblical teachings for
helping those who want to learn the beautiful art of being and
becoming all that God intends in their marriage.

Lysa TerKeurst

President, Proverbs 31 Ministries
Author, *Capture His Heart* and *Capture Her Heart*

focus on the family® marriage series

the
giving
marriage

Gospel Light

Gospel Light is an evangelical Christian publisher dedicated to serving the local church. We believe God's vision for Gospel Light is to provide church leaders with biblical, user-friendly materials that will help them evangelize, disciple and minister to children, youth and families.

It is our prayer that this Gospel Light resource will help you discover biblical truth for your own life and help you minister to others. May God richly bless you.

For a free catalog of resources from Gospel Light, please call your Christian supplier or contact us at 1-800-4-GOSPEL *or* www.gospellight.com

PUBLISHING STAFF
William T. Greig, Chairman
Kyle Duncan, Publisher
Dr. Elmer L. Towns, Senior Consulting Publisher
Pam Weston, Senior Editor
Patti Pennington Virtue, Associate Editor
Hilary Young, Editorial Assistant
Jessie Minassian, Editorial Assistant
Bayard Taylor, M.Div., Senior Editor, Biblical and Theological Issues
Samantha A. Hsu, Cover and Internal Designer
Carol Stertzer, Contributing Writer

ISBN 0-8307-3151-2
© 2003 Focus on the Family
All rights reserved.
Printed in the U.S.A.

table of contents

foreword

The most urgent mission field on Earth is not across the sea or even across the street—it's right where you live: in your home and family. Jesus' last instruction was to "make disciples of all nations" (Matthew 28:19). At the thought of this command, our eyes look across the world for our work field. That's not bad; it's just not *all*. God intended the home to be the first place of Christian discipleship and growth (see Deuteronomy 6:4-8). Our family members must be the *first* ones we reach out to in word and example with the gospel of the Lord Jesus Christ, and the fundamental way in which this occurs is through the marriage relationship.

Divorce, blended families, the breakdown of communication and the complexities of daily life are taking a devastating toll on the God-ordained institutions of marriage and family. We do not need to look hard or search far for evidence that even Christian marriages and families are also in a desperate state. In response to the need to build strong Christ-centered marriages and families, this series was developed.

Focus on the Family is well known and respected worldwide for its stead-fast dedication to preserving the sanctity of marriage and family life. I can think of no better partnership than the one formed by Focus on the Family and Gospel Light to produce the *Focus on the Family Marriage Series*. This series is well-written, biblically sound and right on target for guiding couples to explore the foundation God has laid for marriage and to see Him as the role model for the perfect spouse. Through these studies, seeds will be planted that will germinate in your heart and mind for many years to come.

In our practical, bottom-line culture, we often want to jump over the *why* and get straight to the *what*. We think that by *doing* the six steps or *learning* the five ways, we will reach the goal. But deep-rooted growth is slower and more purposeful and begins with a well-grounded understanding of God's divine design. Knowing why marriage exists is crucial to making the how-tos more effective. Marriage is a gift from God, a unique and distinct covenant relationship through which His glory and goodness can resonate, and it is only through knowing the architect and His plan that we will build our marriage on the surest foundation.

God created marriage; He has a specific purpose for it, and He is committed to filling with fresh life and renewed strength each union yielded to Him. God wants to gather the hearts of every couple together, unite them in love and walk them to the finish line—all in His great grace and goodness.

May God, in His grace, lead you into His truth, strengthening your lives and your marriage.

Gary T. Smalley
Founder and Chairman of the Board
Smalley Relationship Center

introduction

*At the beginning of creation God "made them male and female." "For this
reason a man will leave his father and mother and be united to his wife,
and the two will become one flesh." So they are no longer two, but one.*
Mark 10:6-8

The Giving Marriage can be used in a variety of situations, including small-
group Bible studies, Sunday School classes or counseling or mentoring
situations. An individual couple can also use this book as an at-home
marriage-building study.

Each of the four sessions contains four main components.

Session Overview

Tilling the Ground
This is an introduction to the topic being discussed—commentary and questions to direct your thoughts toward the main idea of the session.

Planting the Seed
This is the Bible study portion in which you will read Scripture and answer
questions to help discover lasting truths from God's Word.

Watering the Hope
This is a time for discussion and prayer. Whether you are using the study at
home as a couple, in a small group or in a classroom setting, talking about
the lesson with your spouse is a great way to solidify the truth and plant it
deeply into your hearts.

Harvesting the Fruit
As a point of action, this portion of the session offers suggestions on putting
the truth of the Word into action in your marriage relationship.

Suggestions for Individual Couple Study

There are at least three options for using this study as a couple.

- It may be used as a devotional study that each spouse would study individually through the week; then on a specified day, come together and discuss what you have learned and how to apply it to your marriage.
- You might choose to study one session together in an evening and then work on the application activities during the rest of the week.
- Because of the short length of this study, it is a great resource for a weekend retreat. Take a trip away for the weekend, and study each session together, interspersed with your favorite leisure activities.

Suggestions for Group Study

There are many ways that this study can be used in a group situation. The most common way is in a small-group Bible study format. However, it can also be used in adult Sunday School class. However you choose to use it, there are some general guidelines to follow for group study.

- Keep the group small—five to six couples is probably the maximum.
- Ask couples to commit to regular attendance for the four weeks of the study. Regular attendance is a key to building relationships and trust in a group.
- Encourage participants *not* to share anything of a personal or potentially embarrassing nature without first asking the spouse's permission.
- Whatever is discussed in the group meetings is to be held in strictest confidence among group members only.

There are additional leader helps in the back of this book and in *The Focus on the Family Marriage Ministry Guide.*

Suggestions for Mentoring or Counseling Relationships

This study also lends itself for use in relationships where one couple mentors or counsels another couple.

- A mentoring relationship, where a couple that has been married for several years is assigned to meet on a regular basis with a younger couple, could be arranged through a system set up by a church or ministry.
- A less formal way to start a mentoring relationship is for a younger couple to take the initiative and approach a couple that exemplify a mature, godly marriage and ask them to meet with them on a regular basis. Or the reverse might be a mature couple that approaches a younger couple to begin a mentoring relationship.
- When asked to mentor, some might shy away and think that they could never do that, knowing that their own marriage is less than perfect. But just as we are to disciple new believers, we must learn to disciple married couples to strengthen marriages in this difficult world. The Lord has promised to be "with you always" (Matthew 28:20).
- Before you begin to mentor a couple, first complete the study yourselves. This will serve to strengthen your own marriage and prepare you for leading another couple.
- Be prepared to learn as much or more than the couple(s) you will mentor.

There are additional helps for mentoring relationships in *The Focus on the Family Marriage Ministry Guide.*

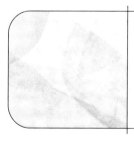

The Focus on the Family Marriage Series *is based on Al Janssen's* The Marriage Masterpiece *(Wheaton, IL: Tyndale House Publishers, 2001), an insightful look at what marriage can—and should—be. In this study, we are pleased to lead you through the wonderful journey of discovering the joy in your marriage that God wants you to experience!*

dealing with an
unfaithful *spouse*

Go, show your love to your wife again, though she is loved
by another and is an adulteress. Love her as the Lord
loves the Israelites, though they turn to other gods.

Hosea 3:1

In his book *The Marriage Masterpiece*, Al Janssen tells the story of a young pastor named Joe who found his long-lost childhood love, Georgine, living as a prostitute on the streets of a big city. Joe loved Georgine so much that he convinced her to leave her lifestyle and become his wife. Although Joe loved Georgine unconditionally, his church didn't accept her, and she felt the bitter sting of rejection. After a couple of years, Georgine began to long for her old, more exciting life, so she left Joe and their children to return to prostitution. This poignant vignette ends with Joe searching for Georgine and finding her once again in the city where he had found her several years earlier. Despite her unfaithfulness, Joe went to great lengths to free Georgine from her sinful life and bring her home.[1]

The word "unfaithful" arouses strong feelings in most of us. The following is the definition of "unfaithful":

> (1) not true to a promise, vow, etc.; (2) not true to a wife, husband, lover, etc., esp. in having sexual intercourse with someone else; (3) inaccurate; inexact; unreliable; untrustworthy.[2]

As you can see, sexual infidelity is only one aspect of being unfaithful. In this session, we're going to take a look at what it means to be unfaithful to your spouse and how Christ has set the ultimate example of faithfulness in all areas of marriage in His loving devotion to His Bride.

tilling the ground

The story of Joe and Georgine is a modern adaptation of Hosea's story in the Old Testament as recorded in the book of Hosea. Hosea was a prophet of God to the nation of Israel. His marriage and subsequent difficulties with his wife, Gomer, are a picture of God's relationship with unfaithful Israel.

1. If you were a member at Joe's church, what would you have thought about his decision to marry Georgine?

    What advice would you have given him?

2. Have you ever been criticized by other believers for doing something that was perceived as irresponsible, even though you knew you were doing what God wanted you to do? If so, what did it feel like?

3. Besides sexual infidelity, what are some other ways that a person could be unfaithful to his or her spouse?

    Let's explore more of Hosea's story and God's heart toward His people.

planting the seed

The book of Hosea relates an emotional and complex story of betrayal of a covenant relationship. Hosea was a prophet who lived during an era of extreme immorality and sinfulness in Israel (793-753 B.C.)[3] Hosea's marriage to Gomer paints a picture of God's love for His people, despite their unfaithfulness.

4. In Hosea 1:2-3, God instructed Hosea to marry an adulterous wife. Why do you think God asked him to do that?

5. According to Hosea 1:4-6,8-9, Gomer gave birth to three children: Jezreel, which means "to scatter"; Lo-Ruhamah, meaning "not loved"; Lo-Ammi, "not my people." Names in the Bible have significant meaning. Hosea means "salvation."[3] How do these names indicate God's feelings toward His people?

Notice the opening instruction to Hosea in 2:1: "Say to your brothers, 'My people,' and of your sisters, 'My loved one'"—the exact opposite of the names of the second and third child! He was addressing His beloved with words of affirmation. The rest of chapter 2 is God's indictment that He instructed Hosea to deliver to the Israelites.

6. What charges did God bring against Israel in Hosea 2:2-13?

What did God tell them He would do as a result of their unfaithfulness?

7. In verse 14, the tone of God's message changes. What does He promise to His Bride?

8. According to Hosea 2:19-20, what qualities should mark every marital union?

9. Why do you think God didn't give up on the Israelites?

10. What does His love for them reveal about His love for you?

11. In what ways is the Church today often unfaithful to God?

Get Outta Here, Satan!

Scripture has a lot to say about faithfulness in marriage. The apostle Paul urged believers to flee from sexual immorality. "All other sins a man commits are outside his body, but he who sins sexually sins against his own body" (1 Corinthians 6:18).

12. In 1 Corinthians 6:15-20, why did Paul point out that Christians are one with Christ in spirit? How does that relate to his command to "flee from sexual immorality"?

How might this revelation affect an it's-not-hurting-anyone attitude about committing adultery or other sexual sins?

Satan's scheme is to gradually lower our standards and seduce us so that we spend less time with the Lord and other worthwhile pursuits, allowing more time to entertain tempting thoughts. It may begin by going to lunch with a coworker of the opposite gender or watching a movie that plants lustful thoughts in our minds.

Recent studies showed that Americans spend $8 billion on hard-core pornographic videos, peep shows, live sex acts, adult cable programming, computer pornography, sexual devices and sex magazines.[4] As a culture we are obsessed with sexual attraction. Is it any wonder that so many marriages are in trouble?

13. According to James 1:13-14, what happens when a person gives in to temptation?

To what does sin give birth (v. 15)?

14. What things tempt you the most?

15. How do you usually handle temptation?

Have you been honest with your spouse about your temptations?

16. Are you able to listen to your spouse talk about his or her temptations without being judgmental or disruptive?

Once you and your spouse are able to share your daily struggles and temptations with each other, you will experience a deeper level of honesty and openness. Any time a person admits his or her temptations, it pops the balloon, so to speak. The thought of that particular temptation becomes less exciting.

Pray often with your spouse that the Lord will help each of you walk uprightly before Him. Let this verse be your inspiration:

Whatever is true, whatever is noble, whatever is right, whatever is pure, whatever is lovely, whatever is admirable—if anything is excellent or praiseworthy—think about such things (Philippians 4:8).

Committing this verse and other similar ones to memory can be the first step in dealing with tempting thoughts or actions.

Adultery Hits Home

As you saw in Hosea, God is merciful. He forgives sinners, and so must we.

Hosea 3 describes Hosea's reconciliation with Gomer. Notice how Hosea's actions are a picture of God's reconciliation with us. Hosea sought out Gomer and paid the price to redeem her, but there was one condition on their reconciliation.

17. What was the condition Hosea put on Gomer's return?

   Was it a reasonable condition? Explain.

Hosea loved and married someone who did not remain faithful. By Jewish law, an adulterous spouse normally would have been sentenced to death by stoning (see Leviticus 20:10), but God used Hosea's experience to show how much He loves us who are so deserving of a death sentence for our sin.

18. Consider the biblical example of the woman brought to Jesus for committing adultery. "If any one of you is without sin," Jesus told the Pharisees, "let him be the first to throw a stone at her" (John 8:7). To the woman, he said with compassion, "Go now and leave your life of sin" (v. 11). How does that relate to the condition Hosea placed on Gomer's return to their marriage?

Sometimes it is easier to accept God's forgiveness than it is to forgive ourselves when we sin. Rather than *condemn* yourself for your sinful behavior, *change* your behavior. That's what God desires. He wants you to walk away from temptation and to experience true freedom.

If your spouse has been unfaithful to you by committing adultery, you have some decisions to make. Contributors to *The Woman's Study Bible* say "a spouse who is able to forgive adulterous behavior on the part of a mate is encouraged to remain within a marriage. [However,] adultery is regarded as such a severe breach of trust and fidelity that it is noted as *permissible* grounds for divorce"[5] (see Matthew 5:32; 19:9).

Likewise, Al Janssen states in his book that a spouse doesn't have to "endure endless infidelity. . . . Jesus Himself acknowledged that adultery was the one legitimate grounds for divorce, at least when the offender continues unrepentant."[6]

19. Why is adultery such a betrayal of trust in a marriage?

20. Do you know of someone who has dealt with the issue of adultery in his or her marriage? What were the consequences of unfaithfulness?

21. What can a couple do to guard against the temptation of having an affair?

22. What can we do to guard our hearts from lustful thoughts or sexual immorality?

23. Think about people you know who have committed adultery. What do you think led to their unfaithfulness?

Sexual immorality has wrecked numerous homes and created emotional turmoil for many families. If you have been faithful and your partner has not, you know how Hosea must have felt. In fact, you have a taste of how God must have felt—and still feels today. If you are presently in this situation, pray that you will hear clearly from the Lord. You may need to separate yourself from your spouse for a time to gain a fresh perspective on the situation. You should also seek outside help from a Christian counselor who can give you objective guidance in reestablishing a trustworthy relationship.

Note: *In additional to spiritual issues, there are some legitimate health concerns related to adultery. A woman I know is separated from her promiscuous husband. She is praying for God to restore their marriage. Her husband recently told her that he wanted to come back, and she wisely said that if he did, he would have to agree to be tested for HIV and other sexually transmitted diseases.*

Consider Susan's story.

> Susan works for a successful company and deeply respects her boss,
> Kent, who has built the company up from scratch. She is married,
> but he is single. They have a lot in common and their work requires
> that they spend a lot of time together working on specific projects.
> Kent is passionate about his work, and he regularly praises Susan
> for her work performance. Susan's husband, Phil, is quiet and
> reserved and finds it difficult to express his feelings and needs, but
> the two of them do share many of the same interests. In spite of her
> love for Phil, Susan has begun to feel more valued and appreciated
> at work than at home, and she especially enjoys her conversations
> with Kent. As she sat down one weekend and analyzed her situa-
> tion, she realized she was becoming emotionally attached to Kent
> and could easily slip into an affair with him.[7]

24. In your opinion, how common is this scenario?

25. If you were Susan, what would you do?

If you were Kent and sensed Susan's emotional attachment, what would you do?

26. If Phil suspects that Susan is becoming emotionally involved with Kent, what should he do?

27. What safeguards can a couple establish to avoid work-related emotional affairs that might lead to adultery?

28. How do you think God views emotional affairs?

First, discuss your answers to questions 14 through 16 with your spouse.

29. Think of small ways in which you may have been unfaithful to your spouse. Did you recently say something negative about him or her in public? Have you been making more time for the kids' activities than you have been reserving for your spouse? Have you been spending too much time at work or with friends?

Ask your mate for forgiveness, and seek to be faithful in all ways. Give your spouse permission to tell you the next time you behave in a way that projects unfaithfulness—and don't be offended to receive the news. After all, unfaithfulness in seemingly small ways can easily lead to sexual infidelity.

To avoid lustful thoughts, guard your heart from sexually suggestive or explicit videos, movies, novels, magazines, radio and television programs and Internet sites. These items may cause you to stumble and lead you down the path of temptation into sin. Get rid of all questionable products in your home, and replace them with reading and viewing materials that will draw you closer to God and your spouse. Do you have a problem with Internet pornography? Ask your spouse to help keep you accountable. Install a filter to block inappropriate sites and related garbage. It might even require that you get rid of those things that cause temptation to enter your home and your thoughts.

Find an accountability partner of the same gender. An accountability partner should be someone who has a heart for serving the Lord and will keep matters confidential. Meet weekly, biweekly or monthly to pray for one another. Discuss and pray about all areas of unfaithfulness that are keeping you from enjoying a deeper relationship with God and your spouse.

Pray with your spouse, asking the Lord's help in staying faithful in your marriage. Keep short accounts of your sins with Him and with your spouse whenever you have a problem remaining faithful to your commitment to your spouse.

Note: If you are experiencing serious problems with issues of trust and faithfulness in your marriage, we advise you to seek professional help through a reputable Christian counselor. Your pastor may be able to guide you in finding the right person, or you can call Focus on the Family's counseling department (1-800-A-Family or 1-719-531-3400) for a free consultation by a licensed counselor[8] and a referral to a national counseling service network of over 2,000 licensed counselors throughout the United States.

Notes

1. Al Janssen, *The Marriage Masterpiece* (Wheaton, IL: Tyndale House Publishers, 2001), pp. 115-136.
2. *The Collins English Dictionary,* www.wordreference.com (accessed December 4, 2002), s.v. "unfaithful."
3. Dorothy Kelley Patterson and Rhonda Kelley, eds., *The Woman's Study Bible: Opening the Word of God to Women* (New King James Version) (Nashville, TN: Thomas Nelson, Inc., 1995), p. 1456.
4. Ed Young, *Fatal Distractions* (Nashville, TN: Thomas Nelson, Inc., 2000), p. 119.
5. Patterson and Kelley, *The Woman's Study Bible*, p. 1462.
6. Al Janssen, *The Marriage Masterpiece*, pp. 128-129.
7. This is a compilation of several stories. Any resemblance to an actual situation is purely coincidental.
8. Counselors at Focus on the Family are licensed in the state of Colorado.

living with an unbelieving *spouse*

If any brother has a wife who is not a believer and she is willing to live with him, he must not divorce her. And if a woman has a husband who is not a believer and he is willing to live with her, she must not divorce him.

1 Corinthians 7:12-13

When I was a girl, my family went to church nearly every time the door was open: Sunday mornings, Sunday nights and Wednesday nights. I remember feeling sorry for the married women who attended without their husbands. At the same time, I admired them for their faithfulness. Some of them came with their children and sat by themselves as the children performed in the annual Christmas musical. Even then, I sensed how important it was to marry a believer, and if I was going to get married, I wanted a spiritual close-ness much like my parents had.

Fortunately, I did marry a Christian. We attend church together and can relate on most spiritual matters.

For one reason or another, some of you may not be spiritually connected to your spouse. Don't give up the dream! God wants you to persevere, to keep believing for the salvation of your unbelieving spouse and to stay put in the marriage. You may be the only *Jesus* your spouse sees!

Whether your spouse is not a believer or is simply facing a time of spiri-tual rebellion, this study is designed to help keep you on track and stay com-mitted to what God's Word says about this topic.

tilling the ground

Because God specially designed us with a body, soul and spirit, it's not surprising that spiritual matters play such a huge role in marriage. Think about it: Even people who don't claim to believe in God can become very emotional when spiritual topics are discussed.

1. Why might a person's religion be so important in a marriage relationship?

2. Why would unbelievers be attracted to Christians?

3. Why would a Christian be attracted to an unbeliever?

4. What characteristics attracted you to your spouse?

5. Even if both spouses are Christians, there might be areas where there is a spiritual mismatch. What, if any, spiritual concerns do you and your spouse differ on?

According to Dr. Fred Lowery, author of *Covenant Marriage*, if you are married to an unbeliever, you have *union* but no *unity*. "There is no agreement at the deepest level of the spirit," he writes.[1] Christ cannot be at the center of a marriage unless both parties put Him there.

planting the seed

God's perfect plan is for a believer to marry someone who loves and serves Him. The apostle Paul admonished us in 2 Corinthians 6:14: "Do not be yoked together with unbelievers. For what do righteousness and wickedness have in common?"

Sometimes in our disobedience, we ignore the voice of the Holy Spirit and give in to our own desires. Even Paul, one of the greatest evangelists of all times, experienced this internal struggle. "So I find this law at work: When I want to do good, evil is right there with me," he said. "For in my inner being I delight in God's law; but I see another law at work in the members of my body, waging war against the law of my mind and making me a prisoner of the law of sin at work within my members" (Romans 7:21-23).

As some may have discovered, there is often a price to pay for ignoring God's wisdom. But there is hope for those who have stepped outside of God's will.

6. What are the usual reasons that believers marry unbelievers?

7. What often happens when believers ignore God's mandate and marry unbelievers?

8. What advice would you give a Christian friend deeply in love with a seemingly *good* person who doesn't have a relationship with Christ?

Whether we are stepping outside God's will in choosing our marriage partner or in making wrong choices in other areas of our life, there will be consequences to our actions. When we return to God and repent, He is merciful and forgiving, but we must still live with the consequences of past choices. He will provide the strength and grace to live victorious in spite of our circumstances.

First Comes Love; Then Comes . . . Christianity?

The climate of a marriage can quickly change when two unbelievers marry and one later becomes a Christian. Consider the example of noted authors Lee and Leslie Strobel, who wrote *Surviving a Spiritual Mismatch in Marriage*. When Leslie became a believer, Lee said their fairy-tale marriage took a nose-dive—at least for him. He was afraid he was going to lose his wife to Jesus Christ.[2]

Leslie wisely heeded the biblical advice found in 1 Peter 3:1: "Wives, in the same way be submissive to your husbands so that, if any of them do not believe the word, they may be won over without words by the behavior of their wives."[3]

Leslie made certain that she was attentive to her husband and his needs. Although there were new conflicts that arose because of her newfound faith, she made it a point not to preach to him and instead focused on the activities they had in common. Ultimately, God used Leslie to point Lee to Christ.

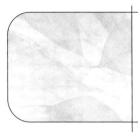

> **Note:** *If an unbelieving spouse is involved in adultery or other wicked behavior, the situation becomes more complex. It is advised that you seek professional Christian counseling to deal with such a serious situation. (See p. 23 at the end of session 1 for further information.)*

9. What does 1 Corinthians 7:12-16 say about being married to an unbeliever who is willing to live with the believing spouse?

10. Look closely at verse 15. What do you think is meant by "God has called us to live in peace"? What should a believer do if he or she is married to a physically or emotionally abusive person?

11. One of the biggest obstacles in a spiritually mismatched marriage is how to raise the children. How might verse 14 be an encouragement to a believer married to an unbeliever?

12. What might a believer do if the unbelieving spouse asks him or her to do things that would displease God?

Show—Don't Tell

Those who try to evangelize and shove Jesus down the throat of their unbelieving spouse will likely encounter increased resistance—and may even make things worse. Have you heard the saying "Show—don't tell"? Sometimes it's best to demonstrate the love of Jesus through our actions, not just through our words—and that is exactly what Peter is talking about in 1 Peter 3:1.

Peter goes on to say in verse 4 that a woman's beauty "should be that of your inner self, the unfading beauty of a gentle and quiet spirit, which is of great worth in God's sight."

13. What are things that can be done to develop the inner beauty spoken of in 1 Peter 3?

14. Even in a marriage where both spouses are believers, the spouses still need to show Jesus' love to each other. List some practical ways that you can daily show the love of Christ to your spouse.

15. Read about the fruit of the Spirit in Galatians 5:22-23. Which fruit do you need to develop more fully in relation to your spouse?

16. Can you recall an occasion when your Christlike actions opened doors for you to share your faith with someone? Describe the experience.

How did that experience affect you?

17. Have you ever felt that you missed an opportunity to share Jesus with someone? Describe what happened.

Confront in Love

As we previously read in Romans 7, Christians do struggle with sin—and, unfortunately, we will have inner battles until Christ comes. Why? Because we are imperfect and live in an imperfect world. There may be times when even a believing, committed Christian will make bad choices and fall into a spiral of sin.

The Bible contains numerous examples of godly men and women who were disobedient and made wrong choices. Consider David, who committed adultery with Bathsheba. When she became pregnant, David had her husband, Uriah, killed in battle (see 2 Samuel 11). It's hard to imagine that a man who loved God so much could be caught up in such wickedness. None of us are immune to the influence of sin.

Nathan, God's prophet, confronted David about his sin. When David finally realized what he had done, he responded: "I have sinned against the Lord" (2 Samuel 12:13). But there were consequences. Despite his fasting and prayers, David's son by Bathsheba died. But God forgave David and continued to use him. In fact, he went down in history as Israel's mightiest king.

There may be times in a believer's life when a rebellious spirit takes over and a spouse heads down the wrong path. You might have to be a Nathan in your spouse's life and confront the sin. This is a situation that should be covered in much prayer and even fasting before a spouse (or anyone else for that matter) is approached and the sin is pointed out. When we do not know how to pray, "the [Holy] Spirit himself intercedes for us" (Romans 8:26).

If you are the one being confronted, how will you react?

18. What are some things a couple can do to foster spiritual growth and lessen the risk for spiritual rebellion?

Whether you are the confronter or the confrontee, you need to rely on the grace and power of God to see you through any time of testing or trial. "Blessed is the man who perseveres under trial, because when he has stood the test, he will receive the crown of life that God has promised to those who love him" (James 1:12).

 watering the hope

Consider the story of Louise and Paul Peppin.

> Louise Peppin was married for 71 years to her unbelieving husband, Paul. He was a good provider and loved his family, but he wanted nothing to do with church. Year after year, Louise prayed that her husband would come to know God—but she never saw that happen.
>
> Although she never saw the results of her prayers, they were not in vain. During the year before Louise's death, Paul suffered a series of strokes and ended up in the hospital in a partial coma. His grandson Bruce went to visit him the day before his grandmother's funeral

and found his grandfather awake and listening intently to what Bruce had to share. Bruce prayed with his grandfather to receive the gift of eternal life through Jesus Christ. Bruce believed that "his grandfather had the experience of the thief on the cross next to Jesus. 'I believe my grandfather acknowledged all that he'd heard over the years and stumbled into the kingdom at the last hour. It's a legacy to the faithfulness of my grandmother.'"[4]

19. Why do you think it took Paul so long to acknowledge Jesus Christ as Lord and Savior?

20. What had he missed out on all those years that he had not followed Jesus?

21. Why do you think Louise did not give up on Paul and just divorce him?

22. How was the family sanctified by Louise's life (see 1 Corinthians 7:12-14)?

23. Do you know of someone like Louise who has prayed for an unbelieving spouse? Describe the effect that person's witness has had on others and, in particular, on you.

Because God has given each of us a free will, we can only pray that our loved ones will make a personal decision for Christ. James 5:16 says, "The prayer of a righteous man is powerful and effective." Consider keeping a prayer journal, recording your requests and the answers to your prayers concerning your spouse. Even if your spouse is a believer, he or she needs your prayerful support. You will be amazed to see how God hears and answers even the smallest of requests.

Ultimately, we all have to decide whom we will serve. Even if your spouse (or other loved ones) never comes to know the Lord, one thing is certain: By weathering the storms and diligently seeking the Father, you will certainly become more like Jesus.

 harvesting the fruit

If this study has touched a nerve in your marriage relationship, you and your spouse will need to deal with the issues it has brought up. That might require professional counseling with your pastor or a Christian counselor.

24. What is the benefit of staying with a spouse who has chosen not to follow the Lord?

25. What are the positive aspects of your marriage that encourage you to stay together?

26. If one of you (or both of you) is not a believer in Christ, what are some issues you need to deal with?

If you and your spouse are both believers, you can be a catalyst to help others who struggle in this area.

27. What would you tell a young person at your church who wants your opinion about dating an unbeliever?

28. Look around you. Are there any church members who come alone because their spouse won't join them? What could you do to encourage and uphold that person? What activities could you and your spouse invite them to if one of them isn't a Christian?

29. How can you strengthen your own marriage to avoid spiritual rebellion?

Be Prepared to Share Christ

Are you prepared to share God's plan of salvation with your spouse or other unbelievers?

What to Share About Christ

- God loves you and wants you to have eternal life (see John 3:16).
- Sin keeps us separated from God (see Romans 3:23; 6:23).
- Jesus paid the penalty for our sin by dying on the cross. Only His death on the cross can bridge the gap between God and people (see 1 Timothy 2:5; Romans 5:8).
- Our response is to receive Christ (see Revelation 3:20; Romans 10:9).

How to Receive Christ

- Admit you are a sinner—this involves confession.
- Be willing to turn from your sins—repent.
- Believe that Jesus died on the cross and rose from the grave.
- Invite Jesus to come in and control your life through the Holy Spirit.

Notes

1. Dr. Fred Lowery, *Covenant Marriage* (West Monroe, LA: Howard Publishing, 2002), p. 76.
2. Lee and Leslie Strobel, *Surviving a Spiritual Mismatch in Marriage* (Grand Rapids, MI: Zondervan Publishing House, 2002).
3. Ibid.
4. Al Janssen, *The Marriage Masterpiece* (Wheaton, IL: Tyndale House Publishers, 2001), pp. 132-133.

living with an
incapacitated *spouse*

*We also rejoice in our sufferings, because we know that suffering produces persever-
ance; perseverance, character; and character, hope.*

Romans 5:3-4

Born in 1950, Joni Eareckson was the youngest of four daughters who grew
up in a loving Christian home. Her close family was very involved in a wide
variety of outdoor activities. Along with her athletic abilities, Joni was also
blessed with creative talents, and having just graduated from high school,
she looked forward to a promising future.

However, one July day in 1967 her life was irrevocably changed. When she
dove into the Chesapeake Bay near her Maryland home, she immediately
realized something was wrong. She had hit the bottom of the bay and broken her neck. As a result of the accident, she was paralyzed from the shoul-
ders down and would spend the rest of her life in a wheelchair with others
taking care of her most basic needs.

While dealing with her anger, severe depression, suicidal thoughts and
the lengthy rehabilitation, Joni began to understand that God had a purpose
for her life. With God's help and the aid and encouragement of family and
friends, Joni's life is full and active. Despite her physical limitations, she is a
best-selling and award-winning author of over 30 books, a highly sought
after speaker, an advocate for disabled people and the founder and director
of Joni and Friends, a ministry that serves disabled people all over the world.
She also has a daily five-minute radio broadcast that is heard on over 850
outlets. She has also become known for her lovely singing voice and the
beautiful pictures that she creates by holding the brush, pen or pencil in her
mouth.[1]

Perhaps the most remarkable part of her story is her marriage to Ken Tada, which took place in 1982. Joni had resigned herself to remaining single all her days until Ken came into her life. They have been happily married now for over 20 years. A recently retired teacher, Ken now works full-time alongside Joni in the Joni and Friends ministry. Ken says, "I love working beside my wife in ministry that involves sharing the good news of Christ with disabled people. It's something I know a lot about!"[2] He was recently the honored recipient of the FamilyLife Ministries Robert McQuilken Award for "The Courageous Love of a Marriage Covenant Keeper."[3]

Most marriages may not experience quite so serious a disability as the paralysis of one spouse, but every marriage will have its tough times. A spouse might come down with a long-term illness (such as chronic fatigue syndrome) or experience a short-term injury or illness (such as a back injury or pneumonia) that requires an extended time of convalescence. Even clinical depression can have a negative impact on a marriage. Any difficulty or trial has the potential to adversely affect a marriage relationship, but God has made His power available to help any couple triumph over any adversity.

 tilling the ground

When we plan our weddings, most of us do not anticipate trials or difficulties. However, if we said the traditional vows at our ceremony, we vowed to stay together through the good and the bad.

1. What do the vows "for better or for worse, for richer or for poorer, in sickness and in health" mean to you?

2. In what ways might a debilitating illness or injury impact a person's identity and self-worth?

How would damaged self-esteem impact a marriage relationship?

3. Have you or someone you know experienced a situation where a spouse has been temporarily or permanently incapacitated? How has that impacted the marriage?

Even situations such as the death of a relative or being passed over for a job can cause temporary setbacks in your life and affect your marriage. Knowing that trials are a part of every life and being prepared to deal them are important in building a strong marriage.

 *planting* the seed

Refined by Fire

God never said it would be easy for us as Christians. In fact, Paul said we will experience trials but that these trials have a purpose: "We know that suffering produces perseverance; perseverance, character; and character, hope" (Romans 5:3-4). The apostle Peter wrote, "In this you greatly rejoice, though now for a little while you may have had to suffer grief in all kinds of trials. These have come so that your faith—of greater worth than gold, which perishes even though refined by fire—may be proved genuine and may result in praise, glory and honor when Jesus Christ is revealed" (1 Peter 1:6-7). God allows us to experience adversity and heartache, but He will bring out something positive when we are surrendered to Him.

4.   How can suffering ultimately lead to hope, as Paul described in Romans 5:3-4?

5.   Reread 1 Peter 1:6-7. Have you seen the evidence in your own life or in the lives of others where difficulties or troubles have resulted in a pure-gold faith? Explain.

The process of refining gold or silver requires very high heat. When the gold or silver is melted, the impurities rise to the surface where they can be skimmed off by the gold- or silversmith. That is a picture of what God does for us through adversity—He skims off those things that make us impure.

Built on a Strong Foundation

Matthew 7:24-27 relates the story of the wise builder and the foolish builder.

6.   What is the requirement for a strong foundation in our lives?

Is it easier to build on rock or on sand? How does that relate to facing adversity?

7. How could a couple strengthen the foundation of their marriage?

8. What storms has your marriage weathered so far?

   What has helped you weather these storms?

9. One of Joni Eareckson Tada's favorite verses is 2 Corinthians 12:9: "My grace is sufficient for you, for my power is made perfect in weakness." How has her life demonstrated this principle?

   How does that verse impact you?

The words in 2 Corinthians 12:9 were stated by the Lord to Paul in answer to his prayers asking to have a thorn in the flesh removed from him. No one knows what the thorn might have been, but it caused Paul a great deal of suffering (see v. 7). What ever it might have been, the Lord did not remove it so that Paul might learn to rely on Christ's power to accomplish His plan. We might ask God to remove a difficulty from our own lives, but He does not always answer in the way we expect.

10. Reread 2 Corinthians 12:7-10. How have you experienced Christ's power in your weakness?

Where do you need Christ's power right now?

We need to realize that life will bring storms our way, and we need to be prepared for these storms by building our marriage on God's sure foundation, Jesus Christ. When we strengthen our relationship with Him, our marriage will be stronger and will hold up under the daily pressures no matter the circumstances.

Covered in Prayer

A woman wrote a letter to *Marriage Partnership* magazine asking how she could help her husband, who may have multiple sclerosis (MS). The symptoms, she said, have really taken a toll on him.

Gary and Carrie Oliver, who specialize in marriage and family issues, responded to her question. They suggested that "much of a man's identity is based on his ability to do 'manly' things: to provide, procreate, and protect."[4] It is normal for a man to feel a wide range of emotions in such a difficult situation, and they encouraged the writer to identify her own emotions so that she could interact better with her husband. The counselors also encouraged her to contact a local MS support group in her area.[5]

In conclusion they said it was essential to ask other couples to pray for her and her spouse daily and with them regularly. They referred her to James 5:16, which states: "The prayer of a righteous man is powerful and effective."[6]

The Olivers also wrote: "We're not being glib or 'spiritualizing' when we emphasize the power of prayer. It's transformed our own marriage and for more than 30 years we've seen what prayer can do in the lives of many other marriages and families."[7]

No matter what type of pain you or your spouse may be experiencing, be diligent to pray—together as a couple as often as possible as well as alone. Scripture promises, "This is the confidence we have in approaching God: that if we ask anything according to his will, he hears us. And if we know that he hears us—whatever we ask—we know that we have what we asked of him" (1 John 5:14-15). God loves us and hears our cries for help. He wants us to depend on Him for all things, big or small.

11. What difference would daily praying together make in a marriage?

How often do you and your spouse pray together?

12. What prayers of yours have been answered recently?

13. How has prayer made a difference in your marriage?

In the marriages of others that you know?

Not only can we turn to the Lord in prayer as a couple, but we can also turn to other believers for their prayer support. The Olivers suggested that the woman who wrote to them should seek out an MS support group to help her and her husband weather this terrible storm in their lives. Others who have gone, or are going, through similar circumstances can be of immeasurable help, encouragement and support. If you are going through this study with a small group, this is a great opportunity to build a support group for one another through prayer and encouragement. If you are not in a small group, look around for an opportunity to build a support group of fellow believers.

14. Who can you turn to—outside of your own family—for support, prayer and encouragement in difficult times?

If you can't name at least two other people to whom you could turn in times of trouble, what might you do to nurture supportive relationships?

The importance of prayer cannot be overemphasized. If you don't pray together regularly, decide on an action plan with your spouse now, and work toward making prayer a regular part of your daily schedule. In addition to your own personal needs, remember to pray for couples you know who are going through trials.

The creator made us and knows exactly how we are wired. If there were a problem with our house, we would go to the builder of our house, so why not go to God when an illness or setback impacts us spiritually, emotionally or physically?

watering the hope

Consider the story of Jake and Lil.

Jake had worked hard as an insurance salesman for over 30 years, and he eagerly looked forward to an early retirement at 57. He and his wife, Lil, had planned well and scrimped and saved their money to be prepared for this new stage in their lives. They planned on traveling around the country in their beautiful new motor home and had already mapped out their first journey. Just a few weeks before his retirement, Jake answered his office phone one afternoon and heard Lil's tear-filled voice on the other end.

"Jake," she began, but then her voice broke. After a moment to collect herself, she continued, "The doctor just told me that my X rays show a suspicious shadow on my liver." She began to cry softly. "And he wants me to go in Friday for surgery."

Jake jumped up from his chair and told her that he would be right home.

Their retirement plans were put on hold while they made the rounds of doctors, hospitals and chemotherapy. Against Lil's protests, Jake sold the motor home and told her he really would rather stay home anyway. When Lil lost all of her hair, Jake shaved his own head so that the two could admire their matching heads. Their children marveled at how patient and kind their father had become in his care for their mother.

Finally the doctors told them they could do no more for Lil and that she would have a year or two left to live. Jake planned a short trip for the two of them to the cabin they stayed in on their honeymoon 37 years before. It was a heaven-blessed time for both of them as they fished, prayed, walked, sang and reminisced about their life together. Fifteen short months later, Lil died at home in Jake's tender embrace, surrounded by their children.

When asked how he survived the ordeal, Jake could only say, "She was never a burden to me. It was a blessing to be able to love and care for her the way she had loved and cared for me for 38 years. I know we will be together in heaven one day."[8]

15. What legacy did Jake and Lil's marriage leave for their children and grandchildren?

16. Often our dreams are not carried out the way we planned. How do you react when your plans are cut short or even shattered?

17. How could others minister to couples such as Jake and Lil?

18. Do you know someone like Jake who willingly serves his or her spouse? What have you learned from that marriage model?

Even if you or your spouse never experience a debilitating illness or injury, there will be times when one spouse must give more than his or her 100 percent to the other, such as during illness, grief, depression or other emotional or physical stress. Even happy times—a new baby, a relocation, the holidays, etc.—can put extra stress on a marriage. The deeper we build our marriage foundation on God's Word and a growing relationship with Him, the better we can withstand the storms of life.

19. What do you and your spouse need to do to strengthen your marriage foundation so that you can weather life's storms?

20. What are some of the happy times that have put stress on your marriage?

21. How has your spouse shown compassion, tenderness and love to you during a difficult time? Have you thanked him or her for that support?

22. In what situations do you need to show compassion, tenderness and love toward your spouse?

Do you need to ask forgiveness from your spouse for neglecting him or her during a difficult time? Write down your thoughts here to share later.

23. How could you and your spouse be a support to someone else who might be going through a difficult time in their marriage?

Paul instructed us to "be kind and compassionate to one another, forgiving each other, just as in Christ God forgave you. Be imitators of God . . . and live a life of love, just as Christ loved us and gave himself up for us as a fragrant offering and sacrifice to God" (Ephesians 4:32—5:2). Pray together, asking God to help you to practice kindness, compassion and forgiveness.

Notes

1. Women of Faith, "Joni Eareckson Tada," *History's Women Newsletter*.
   http://www.historyswomen.com/joni.html (accessed January 20, 2003); "About Joni," *Joni and Friends*,
   http://www.joniandfriends.org/tadabio.shtml (accessed January 20, 2003).

2. "Ken And Joni Tada: Twenty Years of Marriage and Serving Together" *Joni and Friends*,
   http://www.joniandfriends.org/root/ken_joni.shtml (accessed January 20, 2003).

3. Ibid.

4. Gary and Carrie Collins, "Couple Counsel," *Marriage Partnership* 19, no. 3 (Fall 2002), p. 21.

5. Ibid.

6. Ibid.

7. Ibid.

8. This is a compilation of several stories. Any resemblance to an actual situation is purely coincidental.

living with a
hopeful heart

All these people were still living by faith when they died. They did not receive the things promised; they only saw them and welcomed them from a distance.

Hebrews 11:13

I recently watched the interview of an amazing man named Garwin Dobbins on *The Austin Awakening*, a TV program that airs on several Christian networks. Garwin has a rare disease that causes his muscles to turn to bone. "It feels like two different people are twisting the inner core of your bones and putting them over an open flame," he explained.[1]

Despite his disease, Garwin said he is thankful for so many things. Referring to his appreciation of sight, Garwin said, "When I look about and see the color, I know He cares for me."[2]

I wasn't quite prepared for what happened after the brief interview. A few men helped Garwin get out of his wheelchair and propped him up to sing. As he stood leaning on a cane for support, he began to sing with a feeble voice the well-known chorus of "I Can Only Imagine" by MercyMe.[3] The lyrics expressed his anticipation of basking in all the glory of Jesus Christ in heaven. Although Garwin's body was racked with pain, he knew that all the anguish of this life would someday melt in the light emanating from Jesus' perfect face. The thought was overwhelming—his song was a natural overflow of the indescribable hope welling up within him.

Though his body is in pain, Garwin Dobbins isn't focused on this life—his hope rests in Jesus and what lies ahead! He isn't worried about his physical health because he knows he will soon have a glorified body in heaven. Garwin has the spirit of a champion.

Do you have Garwin's champion spirit when it comes to your marriage? Not many of us enter into marriage expecting to have an unfaithful, unbelieving or incapacitated spouse. But when wedded bliss turns into a wedded mess, we can turn to Scripture for comfort. In God's Word, we can begin to see the big picture unfold and can be reminded that those who have a personal relationship with Christ will spend eternity with Him in heaven, where there will be no sorrow or pain.

tilling the ground

For nearly 34 of her 37 years of marriage, Laura has served the Lord faithfully while her husband, Ken, has run from Him. They were separated once earlier in their marriage due to Ken's infidelity, but they got back together. Laura has suggested that they go to marriage counseling, but Ken thinks they have a great marriage and won't go.

Despite the circumstances, Laura is committed to hanging in there and making the most of their marriage. She knows her husband loves her and they do have a lot in common and enjoy doing things together. However, they have never experienced the spiritual depth that Christian couples can. Laura is hopeful that they will one day be spiritually united.

Has Laura found much happiness and fulfillment in her marriage? Probably not as she had planned, but she perseveres and continues to pray for her husband. Her focus is on God rather than her circumstances. She has been faithful to Ken and to God, and she hopes things will change. If they don't, she will at least have the assurance of knowing she obeyed God by staying in the marriage.

1. How can a couple who are not united spiritually still have a good marriage?

2. How might a person keep hope alive in difficult times?

3. Do you know someone like Garwin Dobbins who is an encouragement to others in spite of his or her severe pain or difficulty? How has that person encouraged or strengthened your own faith?

When your hope is in the Lord, the difficult circumstances will be easier to bear. Let's look at biblical examples of hopeful hearts for encouragement.

planting the seed

Hebrews 11 is a powerful, hope-filled chapter to read. In a nutshell, this chapter presents biblical heroes who served God, even when it was tough—men and women including Noah, Abraham and Sarah, Moses, Rahab, and the list goes on. Despite their obedience to God that brought on mistreatment, imprisonment, torture, etc., none of them received the full extent of what God had promised—at least not in their lifetime. Their faith was placed in the eternal Father, not on earthly comforts. They knew that God is sovereign and that He has an eternal plan.

By faith, Moses left his comfortable life as the son of Pharaoh's daughter to lead a group of grumbling slaves.

4. What is the definition of "faith" in Hebrews 11:1?

What does that mean to you?

5. Why is it impossible to please God without faith (see Hebrews 11:6)?

6. After reading Hebrews 11:23-28, list the ways in which Moses stepped out in faith.

7. According to Hebrews 11:25-26, what did Moses *choose* to give up and why?

According to verse 27, why did Moses persevere?

If you were placed in a situation such as Moses experienced, do you think you would have given up or persevered? Why?

8. How should the story of Moses give you hope?

9. Why do you think that people—even many Christians—do not put their hope in God?

As leader of the Israelites, Moses endured much hardship as he obediently endeavored to take God's people from slavery to freedom. And the people he was leading were not willing to be led! They whined; they complained; they rebelled; they questioned his leadership. After 40 years of wandering in the wilderness, Moses was not allowed to enter the Promised Land because of his own sin and lack of trust (see Numbers 20:12). Imagine the disappointment he must have felt when he climbed Mount Nebo, and the Lord showed him the land and told him: "This is the land I promised on oath to Abraham, Isaac and Jacob when I said, 'I will give it to your descendants.' I have let you see it with your eyes, but you will not cross over into it" (Deuteronomy 34:4).

Although Moses didn't get to see the Promised Land, God used him to prepare the Israelites for what was ahead. Scripture tells us that "no one has ever shown the mighty power or performed the awesome deeds that Moses did in the sight of all Israel" (Deuteronomy 34:12). Because of his enduring faith, he was included in Hebrews 11, which some people call the Faith Hall of Fame.

10. What does Hebrews 11:39 say about God's promises? What does that mean to you?

Think about the faith of Abraham and Sarah, who struggled with infertility, even though God had promised them a son. When Sarah was first told she was going to have a child past the normal childbearing years, she laughed. But her disbelief turned to faith when she found she *was* pregnant! She had an attitude change, and her faith grew as a result.

Abraham's faith was even more severely tested. According to Matthew Henry, "The greatest trial and act of faith upon record is Abraham's offering up Isaac"[4] (see Genesis 22:1-13). Can you imagine being willing to sacrifice the son you waited a lifetime to have—the son God promised over and over? And what do you think Isaac was thinking as his father laid him on the altar? Don't you know that both of them were relieved when the angel of the Lord told Abraham not to kill Isaac and provided a substitute sacrifice! Abraham was obedient beyond human reason, and God gave him back his son. More significant, He promised to bless Abraham and his descendants (see Genesis 22:17-18).

11. When Abraham died, most of God's promises to him—numerous descendants, possession of the land, all nations of the earth blessed—had not been realized. Does this challenge your faith in God's promises? Why or why not?

Faith has always been the mark of God's servants. As we look at the list of men and women included in Hebrews 11, however, we are reminded that none of them were perfect. Consider Rahab for example. She was a prostitute and a Gentile—a pagan—yet she demonstrated faith and risked her life for God's people (see Joshua 2) and she was rewarded for her faith (see Joshua 6:22-25; Matthew 1:5).

So how are faith and hope connected? In essence, faith means "trust or confidence in what God has promised."[4] "The same things that are the object of our hope," explained Matthew Henry, "are the object of our faith."[5]

An Eternal Hope

While some Bible characters had a happy ending to their stories (see Hebrews 11:5,31,33-34), many others didn't (see vv. 4,35-38). Men and women have for centuries faced persecution because of their faith. They have been put to death, stoned and left destitute for their faith. Yet it was worth it to them because their hope was in the Lord (see vv. 39-40).

12. What do the faithful receive (see Hebrews 11:6,40)?

Maybe you know someone like Laura who has been faithful to God regarding her marriage but hasn't yet experienced the fruit of obedience. It seems unfair, doesn't it? The truth is, even if we serve the Lord faithfully, Scripture doesn't promise believers an easy life, yet we do have hope in God's power and strength to help us endure victoriously until the end. Jesus even warned His disciples on His final night with them before His death: "In this world you will have trouble. But take heart! I have overcome the world" (John 16:33).

13. What did Jesus mean when He said that He has "overcome the world"?

14. What does Romans 8:24-25 say about hope?

What is one area of your life or marriage where you need to hope in the unseen?

15. Romans 8:28 is often quoted to encourage people who are dealing with problems. Does it encourage you? Explain.

Those in marriages where one spouse must give more than 100 percent have their hearts broken time and again. God rewards such faithfulness. The temporary unhappiness you experience on this earth will fade when He welcomes you into heaven and says, "Well done, good and faithful servant!" (Matthew 25:21).

16. Why do you think God allows Christians to suffer, or experience, unhappiness?

17. Have you ever seen something good come out of a marriage that seemed one-sided? Explain.

Whatever your circumstances, it's important to stay committed to God's plan. As Al Janssen stated in *The Marriage Masterpiece*, "If God can take Hosea's marriage and make it a means of ministry to the nation of Israel, then perhaps He can use any marriage where one partner is willing to let God work. Because God isn't willing to give up on His marriage to Israel and the church, I believe He won't give up on any marriage where just one partner is committed to Him."[6]

We've talked about several types of giving marriages throughout this study and concluded that even in times of unhappiness, God intends for us to honor our commitment to Him and our spouse. The hope of what lies ahead far surpasses anything we could ever experience on this earth.

Think about the following example and how you would deal with a situation like this. How would you remain hopeful?

> Seven years ago, Sheila's husband, Kevin, had a brain tumor. His health gradually deteriorated, and he had to quit working. Sheila had to keep her job because they desperately needed her health insurance. While she works, a nurse comes to make sure Kevin has everything he needs. Physically, his cancer has been devastating, but the worst part is the emotional side. The part of the brain that controls Kevin's emotions no longer functions properly, and he is unable to express his feelings. When Sheila hugs him, he doesn't even hug back. He has no idea that Sheila aches to be held lovingly in his arms.[7]

18. What steps can Sheila take to keep hope alive?

19. If you had a debilitating illness like Kevin's and still had your mental faculties, what could you do to keep hope alive?

20. How might a couple cope with the spiritual lows and sense of hopelessness that may accompany such an illness or other terrible circumstance?

21. How could the Church help couples in this kind of situation?

Unfortunately, some churches and many individuals do not know how to respond to couples that are living with difficult circumstances. More often than not, a couple struggling because one spouse is unfaithful, unbelieving or incapacitated—or other difficult family situations—is abandoned by many. The Church needs to respond in practical ways with compassion, love and encouragement.

 harvesting the fruit

When believers suffer, we have an ever-present hope in a loving God who sent His beloved Son to die for us. Even in unhappy or life-changing situations, knowing that God is pleased with our faithfulness to Him can bring hope and lasting joy.

Our prayer for you: "May the God of hope fill you with all joy and peace as you trust in him, so that you may overflow with hope by the power of the Holy Spirit" (Romans 15:13).

22. How has this study made you more aware of the need to be faithful to your spouse and to God in all circumstances?

23. On a scale of 1 to 10 (with 1 being hopeless and 10 being highest hope), how hopeful were you about your marriage before you completed this study? Has there been any change in your level of hope?

24. Now that you've completed the four sessions of *The Giving Marriage*, what steps will you take as a couple to build a stronger foundation for your marriage?

25. How could you help other couples who may need the hope of Christ in their difficult marriage?

Notes

1. Garwin Dobbins, interview by Randy Phillips, *The Austin Awakening*, Day Star Television, December 7, 2002.

2. Ibid.

3. Bart Millard, "I Can Only Imagine" © 2002 Simpleville Music.

4. Matthew Henry, "Commentary on Hebrew 11," *Matthew Henry Concise Commentary on the Whole Bible*, www.crosswalk.com (accessed November 3, 2002).

5. Ibid.

6. Al Janssen, *The Marriage Masterpiece* (Wheaton, IL: Tyndale House Publishers, 2001), pp. 135-136.

7. This is a compilation of several stories. Any resemblance to an actual situation is purely coincidental.

leader's discussion guide

General Guidelines

1. If at all possible, the group should be led by a married couple. This does not mean that both spouses need to be leading the discussions; perhaps one spouse is better at facilitating discussions while the other is better at relationship building or organization—but the leader couple should share responsibilities wherever possible.

2. At the first meeting, be sure to lay down the ground rules for discussions, stressing that following these rules will help everyone feel comfortable during discussion times.

    a. No one should share anything of a personal or potentially embarrassing nature without first asking his or her spouse's permission.

    b. Whatever is discussed in the group meetings is to be held in strictest confidence among group members only.

    c. Allow everyone in the group to participate. However, as a leader, don't force anyone to answer a question if he or she is reluctant. Be sensitive to the different personalities and communication styles among your group members.

3. Fellowship time is very important in building small-group relationships. Providing beverages and/or light refreshments either before or after each session will encourage a time of informal fellowship.

4. Most people live very busy lives; respect the time of your group members by beginning and ending meetings on time.

The Focus on the Family Marriage Ministry Guide *has even more information on starting and leading a small group. You will find this an invaluable resource as you lead others through this Bible study.*

How to Use the Material

1. Each session has more than enough material to cover in a 45-minute teaching period. You will probably not have time to discuss every single question in each session, so prepare for each meeting by selecting questions you feel are most important to address for your group; discuss other questions as time permits. Be sure to save the last 10 minutes of your meeting time for each couple to interact individually and to pray together before adjourning.

    Optional Eight-Session Plan—You can easily divide each session into two parts if you'd like to cover all of the material presented in each session. Each section of the session has enough questions to divide in half, and the Bible study sections (Planting the Seed) are divided into two or three sections that can be taught in separate sessions.

2. Each spouse should have his or her own copy of the book in order to personally answer the questions. The general plan of this study is that the couples complete the questions at home during the week and then bring their books to the meeting to share what they have learned during the week.

    However, the reality of leading small groups in this day and age is that some members will find it difficult to do the homework. If you find that to be the case with your group, consider adjusting the lessons and having members complete the study during your meeting time as you guide them through the lesson. If you use this method, be sure to encourage members to share their individual answers with their spouses during the week (perhaps on a date night).

Session One | Dealing with an Unfaithful Spouse

> *A **Note to Leaders:** This Bible study series is based on* The Marriage Masterpiece[1] *by Al Janssen. We highly recommend that you read chapters 12 and 13 in preparation for leading this study.*

Before the Meeting

1. Gather materials for making name tags; also gather pens or pencils, paper, 3x5-inch index cards and Bibles.
2. Make photocopies of the Prayer Request Form (see *The Focus on the Family Marriage Ministry Guide,* "Reproducible Forms" section) or provide index cards for recording requests.
3. Read through your own answers from the session and mark the ones that you especially want to have the group discuss. Also highlight any key verses you feel are appropriate to share.
4. Prepare slips of paper with references for the verses that you will want someone to read aloud during the session. Distribute these slips as group members arrive, but be sensitive to those who are uncomfortable reading aloud or who might not be familiar with the Bible.
5. Collect items needed for either of the ice-breaker options (see below).

Ice Breakers

1. If this is the first meeting for this couples group, have everyone introduce themselves and tell the group a brief summary of how they met their spouse, how long they have been married and one interesting fact about their spouse. Be sure to remind them not to reveal anything that the spouse would be uncomfortable sharing him- or herself.
2. **Option 1:** Find examples of how unfaithfulness is glamorized by our culture. These might include promotions for movies or TV shows, magazine or newspaper headlines, or magazine or TV advertisements.

Display the examples and invite discussion on how and why our culture glamorizes sexual infidelity.

3. **Option 2:** Bring visual aids that might represent things other than sexual infidelity that might cause spouses to stray away from their marriage commitment. Examples of things to bring might include money, sports equipment, family picture, church calendar or other calendar, a laptop computer, a cell phone, etc. These might be the actual objects or pictures of the objects. Hand one item or picture to each couple (or person if you have enough items) and ask each to explain how that item might relate to a form of infidelity. For example, the money might represent how a person hides money from a spouse or it might represent a spouse who is too wrapped up in work and making money, ignoring the family. The cell phone might represent spending more time with friends than the spouse.

Discussion

1. **Tilling the Ground**—Discuss questions 1 through 3. If you did not do the option 2 ice breaker, you could use that activity instead of merely discussing question 3. If you did do the option 2 ice breaker, skip question 3.

2. **Planting the Seed**—Invite three volunteers to read Hosea 1 through 3 aloud—one volunteer for each chapter—before discussing questions 4 through 11. Continue discussing the remainder of the questions, except questions 14 through 16, which will be discussed by the individual couples during the Harvesting the Fruit time. If some members are willing, invite them to share their answers to question 15 about how they handle temptation. This might be an encouragement to those who don't know how to handle temptation.

4. **Watering the Hope**— The case study and questions in this section will help members bring the Bible study into the reality of their own expectations versus God's plan. Don't neglect this part of the study, as it brings the whole lesson into the here and now, applying God's Word to daily life.

Divide the group by gender to discuss questions 24 through 28. Have the two groups share with the whole group their answers to question 26 about how to safeguard a marriage against affairs.

5. **Harvesting the Fruit**—This section is meant to help the individual couples apply the lesson to their own marriage and can be dealt with in several ways.

   a. Allow the couples one-on-one time at the end of the meeting. This would require space for them to be alone, with enough space between couples to allow for quiet, private conversations.

      If couples have already answered the questions individually, now would be the time to share their answers. Give a time limit, emphasizing that their discussions can be continued at home if they are not able to answer all of the questions in the time allotted.

      If couples have not answered the questions before the meeting, have them answer them together now. This works best when there is open-ended time for the couples to stay until they have completed their discussion and will require that the leaders stay until the last couple has finished.

   b. Instruct couples to complete this section at home during the week after the meeting. This will give them quiet and private time to deal with any issues that might come up and to spend all the time needed to complete the discussion. You will want to follow up at the next meeting to hold couples accountable for completing this part of the lesson.

   c. At times it might be advantageous to pair two couples to discuss these questions. This would help build accountability into the study.

   Allow time for the individual couples to meet together to complete this section of the questions. Encourage each person to find a partner of the same sex within the group to keep him or her accountable regarding faithfulness in marriage.

6. **Close in Prayer**—An important part of any small-group relationship is the time spent in prayer for one another. This may also be done in a number of ways.

   a. Have couples write out their specific prayer requests on the Prayer Request Forms (or index cards). These requests may then be shared with the whole group or traded with another couple as prayer partners for the week. If requests are shared with the whole group, pray as a group before adjourning the meeting; if requests are traded, allow time for the prayer-partner couples to pray together.

b. Gather the whole group together and lead couples in guided prayer.

c. Have individual couples pray together.

d. Split the members into two groups by gender. Have them pray over their marriages, asking that God would reveal any points where they might be acting unfaithfully toward their spouse.

After the Meeting

1. **Evaluate**—Spend time evaluating the meeting's effectiveness (see *The Focus on the Family Marriage Ministry Guide*, "Reproducible Forms" section).

2. **Encourage**—During the week, try to contact each couple (through phone calls, notes of encouragement, e-mails or instant messages) and welcome them to the group. Make yourself available to answer any questions or concerns they may have and generally get to know them. This contact might best be done by the husband-leader contacting the men and the wife-leader contacting the women.

3. **Equip**—Complete the Bible study, even if you have previously gone through this study together.

4. **Pray**—Prayerfully prepare for the next meeting, praying for each couple and your own preparation. Discuss with the Lord any apprehension, excitement or anything else that is on your mind regarding your Bible study material and/or the group members. If you feel inadequate or unprepared, ask for strength and insight. If you feel tired or burdened, ask for God's light yoke. Whatever it is you need, ask God for it. He will provide!

Reminder: In your desire to serve the members of your group, don't neglect your own marriage. Spend quality time with your spouse during the week!

Session Two | Living with an Unbelieving Spouse

Before the Meeting

1. Gather pens or pencils, paper, 3x5-inch index cards and Bibles.
2. Make photocopies of the Prayer Request Form, or provide index cards for recording requests.
3. Read through your own answers from the session and mark the ones that you especially want to have the group discuss. Also highlight any key verses you feel are appropriate to share.
4. Prepare slips of paper with references for the verses that you will want someone to read aloud during the session. Distribute these slips as group members arrive, but be sensitive to those who are uncomfortable reading aloud or who might not be familiar with the Bible.
5. Prepare a brief testimony of how you came to know Jesus as Savior and Lord of your life. Or call a member of the group and ask if he or she would share a brief testimony.

Ice Breakers

1. Invite couples to share how they applied to their marriage relationship what they learned in last week's session.
2. Ask volunteers to share one praise or good thing that happened during the past week. This is a good chance for those who might not always see the good in things to learn how to express gratitude and thanksgiving to God no matter what the circumstance.
3. Share your testimony or invite the member you contacted to share theirs.

Discussion

1. **Tilling the Ground**—Discuss questions 1 through 4 together as a group. Ask couples to briefly discuss question 5 on their own.
2. **Planting the Seed**—Have the group form at least two small groups to discuss questions 6 through 18. You might want to form groups by

gender. Another suggestion is to have couples pair up to form groups of four.

3. **Watering the Hope**—Discuss questions 19 through 23 with the whole group.

4. **Harvesting the Fruit**—Discuss questions 24 and 25 with the whole group. Then allow time for couples to share their answers to the remainder of the questions individually.

   Option: Invite members to pair up and practice sharing Christ. Encourage each couple to reach out to another couple in which one or both of them are not Christians and plan to do something together. Instruct them to focus on getting to know that couple and building a relationship and not merely looking at it as an evangelistic project.

5. **Close in Prayer**—Distribute Prayer Request Forms (or index cards) and allow time for couples to pray together for the requests of the couple whose form they chose. Close the meeting by praying that each member will have an opportunity to share Christ with someone during the week.

Note: Be sensitive to group members who might not know Christ as Savior and Lord. Be available after the meeting to answer any questions they might have concerning their relationship with God. Be open to the Holy Spirit's leading in asking if anyone would like to make a commitment or rededication to the Lord at this time.

After the Meeting

1. **Evaluate**—Spend time evaluating the meeting's effectiveness.

2. **Encourage**—During the week, try to contact each couple and ask them if they have had an opportunity to share Christ. If anyone accepted Christ during the meeting, follow up by making an appointment to meet with him or her. **Caution:** It is best for you and your spouse to meet with individuals together. Or you could meet one-on-one with the person of the same gender.

3. **Equip**—Complete the Bible study.

4. **Pray**—Prayerfully prepare for the next meeting, praying for each couple and your own preparation.

Session Three | Living with an Incapacitated Spouse

Before the Meeting

1. Gather materials for making name tags in addition to extra pens, paper, 3x5-inch index cards and Bibles.
2. Make photocopies of the Prayer Request Form, or provide index cards for recording requests.
3. Read through your own answers from the session and mark the ones that you especially want to have the group discuss. Also highlight any key verses you feel are appropriate to share.
4. Prepare slips of paper with references for the verses that you will want someone to read aloud during the session. Distribute these slips as group members arrive, but be sensitive to those who are uncomfortable reading aloud or who might not be familiar with the Bible.
5. Obtain a newsprint pad, white board, chalkboard or poster board and the appropriate writing instrument.

Ice Breakers

1. Hand a Prayer Request Form (or index card) to each member as he or she enters the room. Encourage them to at least fill in their name and address, even if they don't have any requests. Remind members that everyone needs someone to pray for them, even if there is no specific need.
2. Ask members if they know of any couples seriously impacted by a setback such as an illness, job loss, etc. (question 3). Invite members to share how that particular couple dealt with the situation.

Discussion

1. **Tilling the Ground**—Discuss questions 1 and 2 if there is time.
2. **Planting the Seed**—Discuss questions 4 through 14 with the whole group.

3. **Watering the Hope**—Have each couple pair up with another couple to discuss questions 15 through 18.
4. **Harvesting the Fruit**—Allow time for individual couples to share their answers.
5. **Close in Prayer**—Have couples rejoin the couple with whom they shared the Watering the Hope discussion. Instruct them to swap their prayer requests and spend a few minutes in prayer together. Encourage each couple to call their prayer-partner couple during the week and share any praises or further requests.

After the Meeting

1. **Evaluate**.
2. **Encourage**—During the week, call each couple and ask if they have called their prayer partners. Encourage them as they continue to complete the study.
3. **Equip**—Complete the Bible study.
4. **Pray**—Prayerfully prepare for the next meeting, praying for each couple and your own preparation. Whatever it is you need, ask God for it. He will provide!

Session Four | Living with a Hopeful Heart

Before the Meeting

1. Gather extra pens or pencils, paper and Bibles.
2. Make photocopies of the Prayer Request Form, or provide index cards for recording requests.
3. Make photocopies of the Study Review Form (see *The Focus on the Family Marriage Ministry Guide*, "Reproducible Forms" section).
4. Read through your own answers from the session and mark the ones that you especially want to have the group discuss. Also highlight any key verses you feel are appropriate to share.
5. Prepare slips of paper with references for the verses that you will want someone to read aloud during the session. Distribute these slips as group members arrive, but be sensitive to those who are uncomfortable reading aloud or who might not be familiar with the Bible.
6. If possible, obtain a CD of "I Can Only Imagine" by MercyMe, which can be found on MercyMe's *Almost There* and *Worship Project*. Make sure you have a CD player available to play the song.
7. Obtain a newsprint pad, white board or chalkboard and the appropriate writing instrument.

Ice Breakers

1. **Option 1:** Ask if anyone had an opportunity to share Christ with another person, and if so, invite at least one volunteer to share briefly.
2. **Option 2:** If you were able to obtain a CD of "I Can Only Imagine," play it now. Instruct members to close their eyes and imagine what heaven will be like. Invite volunteers to share what they "saw."

Discussion

1. **Tilling the Ground**—Discuss questions 1 through 3.
2. **Planting the Seed**—Read Hebrews 11 aloud. Discuss questions 4 through 17 with the whole group.

3. **Watering the Hope**—Discuss questions 18 through 21; then have members discuss how the group can do something practical to help a couple that is living in a difficult situation. Write their ideas on the board or newsprint and challenge the group to decide at least one practical way that they could serve that couple. For example, if they chose to help an elderly couple in which one spouse is bedridden, the group might decide to take turns once a week staying with the ill spouse so that the caregiver could enjoy a day shopping.

4. **Harvesting the Fruit**—Invite individual couples to discuss questions 22 through 25. Invite volunteers to share how the Lord has built their faith and given them a sense of hope as a result of this session.

5. **Close in Prayer**—Play the song (or read the lyrics) again. Invite sentence prayers of praise and thanksgiving. For the benediction, ask everyone to read aloud Romans 15:13: "May the God of hope fill you with all joy and peace as you trust in him, so that you may overflow with hope by the power of the Holy Spirit."

After the Meeting

1. **Evaluate**—Distribute the Study Review Forms for members to take home with them. Share about the importance of feedback, and ask members to take the time this week to write their review of the group meetings and then to return them to you.

2. **Encourage**—Call each couple during the next week and invite them to join you for the next study in the *Focus on the Family Marriage Series*.

3. **Equip**—Begin preparing and brainstorming new activities for the next Bible study.

4. **Pray**—Praise the Lord for the work He has done in the lives of the couples in the study. Continue to pray for these couples as they apply the lessons learned in the last few weeks.

Note

1. Al Janssen, *The Marriage Masterpiece* (Wheaton, IL: Tyndale House Publishers, 2001).

Welcome to the Family!

As you participate in the *Focus on the Family Marriage Series*, it is our prayerful hope that God will deepen your understanding of His plan for marriage and that He will strengthen your marriage relationship.

This series is just one of the many helpful, insightful, and encouraging resources produced by Focus on the Family. In fact, that's what Focus on the Family is all about—providing inspiration, information, and biblically based advice to people in all stages of life.

It began in 1977 with the vision of one man, Dr. James Dobson, a licensed psychologist and author of 18 best-selling books on marriage, parenting, and family. Alarmed by the societal, political, and economic pressures that were threatening the existence of the American family, Dr. Dobson founded Focus on the Family with one employee and a once-a-week radio broadcast aired on only 36 stations.

Now an international organization, the ministry is dedicated to preserving Judeo-Christian values and strengthening and encouraging families through the life-changing message of Jesus Christ. Focus ministries reach families worldwide through 10 separate radio broadcasts, two television news features, 13 publications, 18 Web sites, and a steady series of books and award-winning films and videos for people of all ages and interests.

We'd love to hear from you!

For more information about the ministry, or if we can be of help to your family, simply write to Focus on the Family, Colorado Springs, CO 80995 or call 1-800-A-FAMILY (1-800-232-6459). Friends in Canada may write Focus on the Family, P.O. Box 9800, Stn. Terminal, Vancouver, B.C. V6B 4G3 or call 1-800-661-9800. Visit our Web site—www.family.org—to learn more about Focus on the Family or to find out if there is an associate office in your country.

Strengthen and enrich your marriage with these Focus on the Family® relationship builders.

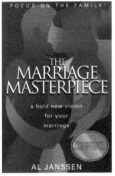

The Marriage Masterpiece

Now that you've discovered the richness to be had in "The Focus on the Family Marriage Series" Bible studies, be sure to read the book the series is based on. *The Marriage Masterpiece* takes a fresh appraisal of the exquisite design God has for a man and woman. Explaining the reasons why this union is meant to last a lifetime, it also shows how God's relationship with humanity is the model for marriage. Rediscover the beauty and worth of marriage in a new light with this thoughtful, creative book. A helpful study guide is included for group discussion. Hardcover.

The Love List

Marriage experts Drs. Les and Leslie Parrot present eight healthy habits that refresh, transform and restore the intimacy of your marriage relationship. Filled with practical suggestions, this book will help you make daily, weekly, monthly and yearly improvements in your marriage. Hardcover.

Capture His Heart/Capture Her Heart

Lysa TerKeurst has written two practical guides—one for wives and one for husbands—that will open your eyes to the needs, desires and longings of your spouse. These two books each offer eight essential criteria plus creative tips for winning and holding his or her heart. Paperback set.

• • •

STRENGTHEN MARRIAGES.
STRENGTHEN YOUR CHURCH.

Here's Everything You Need for a Dynamic Marriage Ministry!

Focus on the Family ® Marriage Series Group Starter Kit
Kit Box • Bible Study/Marriage • ISBN 08307.32365

Group Starter Kit includes:

• Seven Bible Studies: *The Masterpiece Marriage, The Passionate Marriage, The Fighting Marriage, The Model Marriage, The Surprising Marriage, The Giving Marriage and The Covenant Marriage*

• *The Focus on the Family Marriage Ministry Guide*

• *An Introduction to the Focus on the Family Marriage Series* video

Pick up the *Focus on the Family Marriage Series* where Christian books are sold.

Gospel Light

Devotionals for Drawing Near to God and One Another

 Moments
Together
for Couples
Hardcover • 384p
ISBN 08307.17544

 Moments
Together
for Parents
Gift Hardcover
96p
ISBN 08307.32497

 Moments
Together
for Intimacy
Gift Hardcover
96p
ISBN 08307.32489

Give Your Marriage a Checkup

 The Marriage Checkup
How Healthy
Is Your Marriage Really?
Paperback • 140p
ISBN 08307.30699

 The Marriage Checkup
Questionnaire
An Easy-to-Use Questionnaire
to Help You Evaluate the
Health of Your Marriage
Manual • 24p
ISBN 08307.30648

 How to Counsel a Couple
in 6 Sessions or Less
A Tool for Marriage Counseling
to Use in Tandem with the
Marriage Checkup Questionnaire
Manual • 24p
ISBN 08307.30680

Complete Your Marriage-Strengthening Library

 Preparing for Marriage
The Complete Guide
to Help You Discover God's Plan
for a Lifetime of Love
Dennis Rainey
Paperback • 170p
ISBN 08307.17803
Counselor's Pack
(3 books, I Leader's Guide)
ISBN 08307.21568
Couples Pack (2 books) • ISBN 08307.21576
Leader's Guide • ISBN 08307.17609

 Communication:
Key to Your Marriage
A Practical Guide to Creating
a Happy, Fulfilling Relationship
Dr. H. Norman Wright
Paperback • 244p
ISBN 08307.25334
Video Approx. 2 hrs.
UPC 607135.004639

 Holding on to Romance
Keeping Your Marriage
Alive and Passionate
After the Honeymoon Years
Dr. H. Norman Wright
Video • Approx. 1 hr.
UPC 85116.00779